# Justin Bieber

## By Lynn Peppas

# Crabtree Publishing Company

www.crabtreebooks.com

# Crabtree Publishing Company
## www.crabtreebooks.com

**Author:** Lynn Peppas
**Publishing plan research and development:**
  Sean Charlebois, Reagan Miller
  Crabtree Publishing Company
**Project coordinator:** Kathy Middleton
**Photo research:** Crystal Sikkens
**Editor:** Molly Aloian
**Proofreader:** Crystal Sikkens
**Designer:** Ken Wright
**Production coordinator and Prepress
  technician:** Ken Wright

**Photographs:**
Associated Press: pages 8, 11, 21, 25
BigStockPhoto: page 24
Getty Images: Mike Coppola/Stringer: page 13
Keystone Press: PA Wire/PA Photos: cover,
  page 22; BIG Pictures UK: page 7; wenn.com:
  pages 10, 19, 26; Jason L Nelson/AdMedia:
  page 20
Shutterstock: pages 1, 4–5, 6, 9, 12, 14, 18, 23,
  27, 28
Wikimedia Commons: Dhodges: page 15;
  Bped1985: page 17

Every effort has been made to trace copyright holders and to obtain their permission for use of copyright material. The authors and publishers would be pleased to rectify any error or omission in future editions. All the Internet addresses given in this book were correct at the time of going to press. The author and publishers regret any inconvenience caused if addresses have changed or sites have ceased to exist, but can accept no responsibility for any such changes.

**Library and Archives Canada Cataloguing in Publication**

Peppas, Lynn
    Justin Bieber / Lynn Peppas.

(Superstars!)
Includes index.
Issued also in an electronic format.
ISBN 978-0-7787-7607-9 (bound).--ISBN 978-0-7787-7612-3 (pbk.)

    1. Bieber, Justin, 1994- --Juvenile literature.  2. Singers--
Canada--Biography--Juvenile literature.  I. Title.  II. Series:
Superstars! (St. Catharines, Ont.)

ML3930.B545P42 2011        j782.42164092        C2011-905249-0

**Library of Congress Cataloging-in-Publication Data**

Peppas, Lynn.
    Justin Bieber / by Lynn Peppas.
        p. cm. --  (Superstars!)
    Includes index.
    ISBN 978-0-7787-7607-9 (reinforced library binding : alk. paper) --
ISBN 978-0-7787-7612-3 (pbk. : alk. paper) -- ISBN 978-1-4271-8853-3
(electronic pdf) -- ISBN 978-1-4271-9756-6 (electronic html)
    1. Bieber, Justin, 1994---Juvenile literature. 2. Singers--Canada--
Biography--Juvenile literature.  I. Title. II. Series.

ML3930.B54P46 2012
782.42164092--dc23
[B]
                                                        2011029837

## Crabtree Publishing Company
www.crabtreebooks.com          1-800-387-7650

Printed in Canada/082011/MA20110714

**Published in Canada**
Crabtree Publishing
616 Welland Ave.
St. Catharines, ON
L2M 5V6

**Published in the United States**
Crabtree Publishing
PMB 59051
350 Fifth Avenue, 59th Floor
New York, New York 10118

**Published in the United Kingdom**
Crabtree Publishing
Maritime House
Basin Road North, Hove
BN41 1WR

**Published in Australia**
Crabtree Publishing
3 Charles Street
Coburg North
VIC 3058

# CONTENTS

Words that are defined in the glossary are in
**bold** type the first time they appear in the text.

# From Small Town to Big Time

Justin Bieber is a small-town Canadian teen who became one of the biggest superstars in the world. It all started when Justin's mother posted videos of Justin performing on YouTube. She wanted to share the videos with other family members. Little did they know that people other than their family would start watching them, and fall in love with Justin. His fan base grew on YouTube from a few, to a few hundred, to a few thousand, and kept going and growing. Today, millions of fans follow Justin anyway they can: on Twitter, on YouTube, on Facebook, on T.V., in the theater, on the radio, or by buying his music.

Fans even follow Justin in person. These fans are trying to catch the star as he arrives at the MTV Video Music Awards.

## Surprise Story

Justin's early years were pretty normal. He grew up in a small town in the Canadian province of Ontario. He went to school and played sports in his spare time. A lot of people who knew Justin before he became a superstar liked his energy and **enthusiasm** for life. But they never dreamt that he would become the superstar that he is today. Even those closest to Justin didn't know that he wanted to become a professional musician. For a while, Justin and his friends thought he'd make it as a professional athlete. Justin's natural athletic abilities come in handy for his dance moves in concerts and music videos. Today, he's selling millions of albums. He's working with other superstar musicians such as Rascal Flatts and Usher. Ask just about anyone who Justin Bieber is and they'll tell you he's the kid making music and making it big!

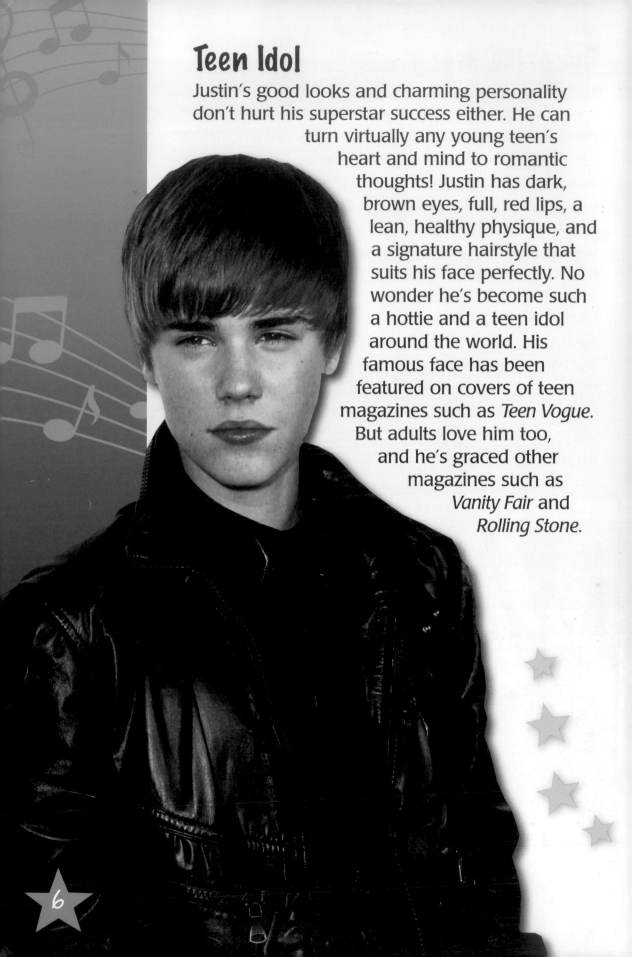

# Teen Idol

Justin's good looks and charming personality don't hurt his superstar success either. He can turn virtually any young teen's heart and mind to romantic thoughts! Justin has dark, brown eyes, full, red lips, a lean, healthy physique, and a signature hairstyle that suits his face perfectly. No wonder he's become such a hottie and a teen idol around the world. His famous face has been featured on covers of teen magazines such as *Teen Vogue*. But adults love him too, and he's graced other magazines such as *Vanity Fair* and *Rolling Stone*.

# Or You Can Call Me...

Fans have come up with all kinds of nicknames for Justin based on his catchy last name. Some call him the "Beeb," or "Bieb." Others call him JBiebz, Biebz, or JB. Even Justin's fans call themselves nicknames using Justin's last name. Many call themselves "beliebers." And there's "Biebermania" which comes from the '60s term "Beatlemania," when the Beatles were the most popular band on Earth. That's un-belieb-able!

## TWEET BIEBER

Justin's whole career was launched with amateur videos on YouTube. Now, he keeps in touch with fans through Facebook and Twitter. At the time this book was written, Justin had close to nine million followers on Twitter. Isn't that Tweet?

Fans who like rhyming nicknames have also been known to catch "Bieber fever."

# The Growing Years: From Toddler to Teen

Justin Drew Bieber was born in London, Ontario, on March 1, 1994. London is a larger city in Southern Ontario with over 300,000 people. Justin grew up in Stratford, Ontario. Stratford is much smaller, with a population of 32,000. The city's claim to fame—besides Justin—is its live professional theater company called the Stratford Shakespeare Festival. Justin says he is proud to be Canadian. He enjoys playing hockey and visiting his Canadian hometown whenever he can.

Justin poses with the Royal Canadian Mounted Police.

8

# Meet Justin's Mom

Justin's mother is Patricia Lynn Mallette, or "Pattie" as most people call her. She was just 18 years old when she found out she was pregnant with Justin. Pattie and Justin's dad, Jeremy Bieber, were going to get married, but they broke up when Justin was 10 months old. Pattie raised Justin on her own in Stratford. She worked hard at low-paying jobs, and she and Justin lived in public housing. The Canadian government offers public housing to people who have financial struggles. Pattie worked hard to try to make sure her only child had everything he needed.

Pattie is a very **spiritual** person. She prays often and believes that God has given her and Justin all the good things in their lives. She raised Justin to be a spiritual person, too.

In an interview, Pattie said that one of the biggest challenges she faced raising Justin was his strong-willed nature. A strong-willed person does what they want to, and doesn't like to bend to the wishes of others. Pattie said she had to stay firm with Justin and not back down. But she did go on to say that being strong-willed is a great leadership quality.

# The Men in Justin's Life

Like Justin's mother, Justin's father was in his teens when Justin was born. After he and Justin's mom broke up he got a job as a construction worker and had to travel out of town for work. Justin said that it "sucked" for him that his Dad was away a lot, but that he understands why he had to do it. Justin also remembers that some of the best times in his life growing up were when his Dad came to his house to play guitar and teach him chords. Justin's grandparents on his mother's side were an

Justin poses with his dad, mom, and half sister.

important part of his life, too. While Justin's mom worked, he often stayed at his grandparents' house. He even had his own bedroom there, decorated with souvenirs from his favorite NHL hockey team, the Toronto Maple Leafs.

Justin is especially close to his grandfather Bruce Dale. He says that his Grandpa has always been there for him whenever he's needed him for as long as he can remember. Bruce says he always thought Justin would become a hockey player, not a peformer.

# Living and Learning

Justin believes in trying new things even though he might not be good at them in the beginning. He says that's how he learned to play music. Justin is a self-taught musician. That means he taught himself how to play music on instruments such as the drums, guitar, trumpet, and piano.

Justin was interested in playing drums when he was just two years old. His mom bought him a toy drum kit and Justin loved it. Later, when he was five years old, his mom's music friends held a benefit at a local bar in Stratford and raised enough money to buy Justin a real drum kit. Justin was "crazy" about it. He still is a drummer to this day. In May 2010, Justin did a drum solo while performing "Baby" on Oprah.

Justin visited Seminole High School, in Florida, where he treated them to a performance on the drums and made a donation to the music program.

11

## School Days in Stratford

Justin started grade 1 at a French immersion school called Jeanne Sauvé Catholic School. Students and teachers in French immersion schools only speak French during classes. Students are immersed, or surrounded, by the French language. Justin attended this school until he was 12 years old. He then attended Northwestern Public Middle School in Stratford. It was not a French immersion school.

Justin now travels with a private tutor who is helping him finish high school. He has five three-hour sessions a week.

### BONJOUR BIEBER

Justin is **bilingual**. That means he can **fluently** speak (or sing) in two different languages, English and French. Canada is a bilingual country. Canada's two official languages are English and French.

WELCOME TO /
BIENVENUE AU
CANADA

### He Said It

*"I want to finish high school and also university and then evolve wherever my music takes me."*
—At a news conference promoting his album *My Worlds Acoustic*

12

*"I didn't dream of becoming a rock star back then. I dreamed of becoming a hockey star…"*
—From *First Step 2 Forever: My Story*

## Justin the Jock

Music isn't Justin's only claim to fame. He's also very athletic. While growing up in Stratford, Justin was involved in sports such as soccer and basketball. But hockey is his all-time favorite sport. His favorite NHL hockey team is the Toronto Maple Leafs. His favorite all-time sports celebrity is hockey player, Wayne Gretzky— The Great One!

## Bieber Buds

It was while playing hockey that Justin met his best friends, Ryan Butler and Chaz Somers. The three have been hanging out since Justin was just eight years old. You can see Justin's friend, Ryan, in his music video for "One Time." In the beginning of the video Justin and Ryan are hanging out playing X-Box at hip-hop singer, Usher's house.

Justin got the opportunity to hold the famous ice hockey trophy, The Stanley Cup.

13

# Million-Viewers Baby!

Justin Bieber went from a small-town "Idol contest" runner-up to a superstar who sells millions of albums and entertains tens of thousands of people in stadiums all over the world. With the help of YouTube, almost everyone on the planet has heard of Justin Bieber!

## Stratford Idol

Justin's interest in music began when he was just a toddler. He kept his love of music a secret from everyone at school. Like most young people, he pretended he was a rock star only when he thought no one else was watching. It was the Stratford Idol competition that changed everything for Justin. Justin competed at age 12, and kept making the elimination cuts until he was competing for first place. He didn't win the competition, but came in second place. The competition gave him his first opportunity to perform for a live audience.

# Taking It to the Streets

Justin had a part-time job when he was 12 years old. But it wasn't a **typical** job such as babysitting or delivering newspapers. Justin used to **busk** on the streets of downtown Stratford for money. Busking is when a person performs on the street, usually singing and playing an instrument. Justin busked on the front steps of the Avon Theatre in Stratford. People walking by would throw a few dollars in Justin's guitar case if they liked his music. His mom or grandpa kept an eye on him across the street and they also recorded videos of him. They posted these on YouTube, as well. After a few hours, on a good day, Justin would make about $200. It was pretty good money for a part-time job doing something he loved!

Justin busked at the Avon Theatre, just as this person is doing.

# Rising Star on YouTube

Justin's popularity on YouTube kept climbing higher and higher. People were watching videos that Pattie had posted and their interest was growing. YouTube views were climbing from hundreds, to thousands, to tens of thousands. It was becoming pretty obvious that a lot of people liked Justin and his singing.

## GROWING PAINS

Justin became known for his high pitch singing voice. However, when puberty hit the Biebs, his voice changed, too, creating a lower singing range. Justin trains every day with his vocal coach, Jan Smith, so that he can still keep hitting the high notes, as well as all the others.

## He Said It

*"It was crazy, because I first put (videos) up and I got a couple of views, then I got 50 and it was cool. Then I got a thousand and I was like, 'What is this? I don't have a thousand family members.' But it kept growing, and… it was like, wow, people started to like me, so I posted some more videos and my fan base kept growing to where I have 90 million views on my YouTube page."*
—In an interview with *Life Story* magazine, December 2010

# He Said It

## Scooter Braun

Justin's videos on YouTube also caught the attention of his future talent manager. Behind every successful superstar there's usually a superstar talent manager. In Justin's case, that manager is Scott Samuel Braun. Scott, who goes by the nickname "Scooter," got Justin Bieber to where he is today. Scooter said it wasn't easy getting Pattie onboard. Pattie was **mistrustful** of people wanting to manage her son's music career. But Scooter kept calling and trying. Pattie and Justin talked it over and finally decided to fly to Scooter's hometown of Atlanta, Georgia, to meet with him. Scooter even introduced her and Justin to members of his own family to help them feel more comfortable. Finally, Justin and his mom couldn't help but 'belieb' in Scooter's vision for Justin.

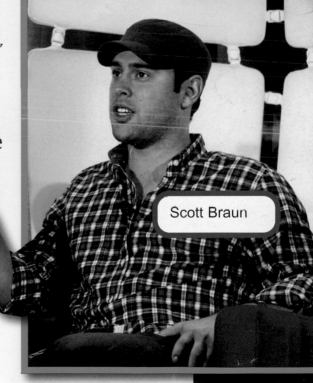

Scott Braun

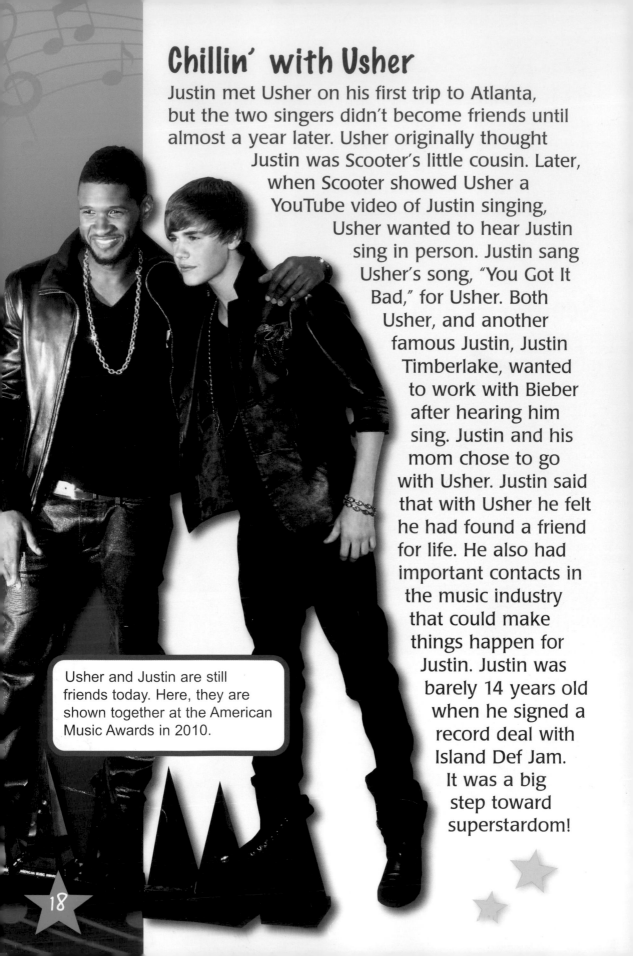

# Chillin' with Usher

Justin met Usher on his first trip to Atlanta, but the two singers didn't become friends until almost a year later. Usher originally thought Justin was Scooter's little cousin. Later, when Scooter showed Usher a YouTube video of Justin singing, Usher wanted to hear Justin sing in person. Justin sang Usher's song, "You Got It Bad," for Usher. Both Usher, and another famous Justin, Justin Timberlake, wanted to work with Bieber after hearing him sing. Justin and his mom chose to go with Usher. Justin said that with Usher he felt he had found a friend for life. He also had important contacts in the music industry that could make things happen for Justin. Justin was barely 14 years old when he signed a record deal with Island Def Jam. It was a big step toward superstardom!

Usher and Justin are still friends today. Here, they are shown together at the American Music Awards in 2010.

# Rockin' My World and My World 2.0

Justin's debut album was an **EP** called *My World*. It came out in the United States and Canada on November 17, 2009. It was also released **internationally**. The record sold 137,000 copies in the United States during its first week. The EP was certified platinum, which means it sold over one million copies in Canada. It went platinum in the U.S. in just two months. In the United Kingdom, it went double platinum, which means it sold two million copies in a year. The album has hit singles such as "One Time," and "One Less Lonely Girl." Justin co-wrote some of the songs for the album with a number of artists and songwriters, such as Usher and The-Dream.

Justin signs copies of his album *My World* at an HMV store in London, England.

*My World* was released as the first part of a two-part album. *My World 2.0* was Justin's first full-length album. It was released four months later on March 23, 2010. *My World 2.0* topped the U.S. Billboard 200 charts at number one in its first week when it sold 283,000 copies. It has gone double platinum in the United States, Canada, and the Philippines. The album has hit singles such as "Baby" featuring rap artist, Ludacris, and "Somebody to Love." On this album, Justin co-wrote all of his songs with other songwriters.

# Falling for the Bieber Charm

Justin said that when he turned 12 years old, he started noticing girls. His first celebrity crush was Beyoncé Knowles. Justin had his first kiss during a competition between him and his friends. They were competing to see who would be the first one to get a kiss from a girl during a school dance. Justin won! On his first official date, Justin took a girlfriend to a buffet restaurant in Stratford.

Today, millions of young people around the world would love the chance to be Justin's love interest. In September 2010, Justin and his "Baby" music video love-interest, Jasmine Villegas, were rumored to have been dating. Even though Justin has never admitted that Jasmine was his girlfriend, the two were photographed kissing in the back seat of a car.

Jasmine Villegas performed as an opening act on Justin's My World Tour 2010.

# Justin and Selena

Since early 2011, Justin has been seen together with Disney's *Wizards of Waverly Place* star Selena Gomez. They went to the 2011 Oscars as a couple in February and shared a kiss at both the Billboard Music Awards in May and the Teen Choice Awards in August. In interviews, the private superstars don't talk too much about their relationship.

Justin and Selena attend Vanity Fair's 2011 Oscar Party.

# You'd Better Belieb It!

Although young **tween** and teen girls make up a large part of Justin's fan base, people from all around the world, male and female, young and old alike, are catching "Bieber fever." Justin can sing, play musical instruments, dance, and act—a combination that's helped him earn the success he enjoys today. There's more to Justin than meets the teenaged eye. He's charming, he's got a good energy, and he's likeable no matter what age you are.

## Bieber Merch

Need a remedy for "Bieber fever"? How about the new Bieber fragrance? It doesn't come in a bottle, like most scents do. Instead, his fragrance called My World comes on a wristband for females, or a dog tag for males. There's also the Bieb's nail polish line called the "One Less Lonely Girl" collection. Nail polish color names are inspired by his songs, such as Step 2 the Beat of My Heart, with heart-shaped glitter inside.

Fans also can purchase Justin Bieber dolls that sing parts of his songs "Baby" or "One Less Lonely Girl," and wear the same outfits from his music videos.

# Trademark Hairstyle

At the beginning of his career, part of Justin's appeal was his thick, sandy brown, pushed-forward hairstyle. His hairstylist, Vanessa Price, created the style for him. He was even known for his signature head toss, that pushed his hair forward. But that all changed in February of 2011 when Justin got a new do with shorter, choppier layers. Justin said he was going for a more mature look. Justin's locks that were cut were saved and sold for charity.

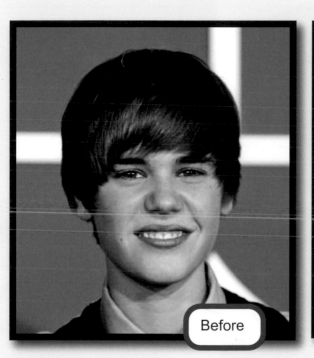

Before

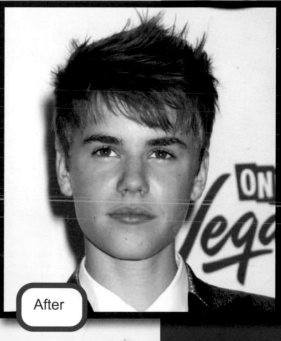

After

## He Said It

*"…I had had [the same haircut] for 3 ½ years, I had just gotten sick of it. It was in my eyes, (and) I didn't want it in my face. I just wanted to change it up."*
—In an interview with Huffpost Entertainment website (www.huffingtonpost.com) February 21, 2011

# The Book on Bieber

In October of 2010, Justin released an autobiography called *First Step 2 Forever: My Story*.

The 240-page book gives details of Justin's life and his rise to fame. Through his own words, and loads of photos, Justin shares with his fans what his life was like growing up in Stratford, ON, and the steps he took to become the superstar he is today. He also lets his readers get a look at what his life is like now, and how he is dealing with his success. Justin's book made it onto *New York Times* best-seller list.

## He Said It

*"I'm excited to share just a little bit more of my world with [my fans] through this book. Between the behind-the-scenes pictures and the story I think this is going to be something they can all enjoy. This is just another way for me to say thank you to my fans.*
—In a press release for *First Step 2 Forever: My Story*

# Bieber on the Big Screen

Fame and fortune go hand-in-hand with television and film appearances. Justin hosted the popular late-night comedy show *Saturday Night Live* with former SNL comedian Tina Fey in April 2010. But his first serious acting role was on the 2010/2011 season premiere of the CBS series *CSI: Crime Scene Investigation*. He played a troubled teen named Jason McCann. In February 2011, Justin returned as Jason McCann and guest starred for a second episode.

Justin Bieber is shown in a scene with Dana Carvey on *Saturday Night Live*.

Justin's biggest role was in the film documentary of his own life called *Justin Bieber: Never Say Never*. The documentary, filmed in 3-D, was released in February 2011. It was about 10 days in Justin's life on his My World Tour.

He also released an album of **remixes** called *Never Say Never* just before the movie. The album has remixes of his songs from *My World 2.0* and features guest artists and bands such as Jaden Smith, Rascal Flatts, Kanye West, and Miley Cyrus. It also included an entirely new song called "Never Say Never," that he worked on with Jaden Smith for the film, *The Karate Kid*.

# World Tour

Justin began his own headlining tour in 2010. He toured venues in Canada and the United States shortly following the release of his *My World 2.0* album. The tour is broken into three sections with two sections in North America, and one in Europe. The North American tour included over 75 shows that began in June 2010 and ended just before Christmas in the same year. During the second section of his North American tour, Justin donated one dollar from every ticket sold to Pencils of Promise, a charity that builds and supplies schools for kids who don't have any. The My World Tour went overseas in March 2011 and included countries such as Switzerland, England, Malaysia, and Australia.

Justin performs in Miami, Florida, during his My World Tour.

26

# And the Award Goes To... Justin Bieber!

Justin Bieber's musical talent is not going unnoticed on the music award scene either. In 2010, Justin won a total of 19 awards. He won four American Music Awards that included Artist of the Year. In 2011, he won numerous awards including six Billboard Music Awards and a Juno Award (Canada's equivalent to a Grammy Award) for Pop Album of the Year. He's even been nominated for a CMT Music Award for his collaboration with Rascal Flatts on the song, "That Should Be Me."

Justin poses with one of his six 2011 Billboard Music Awards.

# Keep Beliebing

Justin started out in a small town in Canada, but he had big dreams that he made come true. Today, people all around the world love his music, and are true Beliebers in Justin's career.

As he tours around the world, Justin is busy writing songs for his next, new album called *Believe*. He's enjoying his fame and fortune and trying not to let it get to his head. It is estimated that Bieber has earned over $100 million dollars in 2010.

ABC television talk show host, Barbara Walters, chose Justin as one of the top 10 most fascinating people of 2010. In an interview with her, Justin said he plans on having a long and successful music career for many more years to come. His secret to staying on top is to remain "grounded." Grounded means you have a good foundation or base in life. The things that keep Justin grounded in his life are his mom, his close friends, and God. Notice that money wasn't in Justin's list of things that keep him grounded!

## He Said It

*"I don't love money, because once you start loving money, you've got a big house and nice cars and just an empty heart, and that's the truth, I'm not just saying that."*
—In an interview in *Rolling Stone* magazine, March 3, 2011

# Timeline

**March 1, 1994**: Justin Drew Bieber is born in London, Ontario, Canada.

**2006**: Justin begins busking in front of the Avon Theatre in Stratford, Ontario, at age 12.

**2008**: Justin signs a record deal with Island Def Jam Music Group at age 14.

**November 17, 2009**: Justin releases debut EP called *My World*. It sells 137,000 copies during its first week of sales in the United States.

**March 23, 2010**: Justin's first full-length album, called *My World 2.0*, is released. It reaches number one on the Billboard 200 during its first week.

**April 2010**: Justin hosts the late-night comedy show, *Saturday Night Live* with comedian Tina Fey.

**June 2010**: Justin begins his My World Tour.

**September 2010**: Justin gets feature role on *CSI: Crime Scene Investigation* television series.

**October 2010**: Justin's autobiography, *First Step 2 Forever: My Story* is published.

**February 2011**: Justin guest stars again on *CSI: Crime Scene Investigation*.

**February 2011**: Justin's album of remixes, called *Never Say Never*, is released on February 14.

**February 2011**: Justin's documentary movie *Justin Bieber: Never Say Never* is released in theaters.

**February 2011**: Justin trades his signature, pushed-forward hairstyle for a shorter, choppier hairstyle.

**February 2011**: Justin Bieber and Selena Gomez attend the Oscars together.

**March 2011**: Justin wins a Juno in Canada for Pop Album of the Year.

**May 2011**: Justin attends the Billboard Music Awards with Selena. He wins six awards.

**August 2011**: Justin and Selena attend the Teen Choice Awards. He wins four and Selena wins five.

# Glossary

**bilingual** The ability to speak and understand two different languages

**busk** To entertain in a public area and receive money donations for performing

**enthusiasm** To be interested in, or be excited about, something

**EP** Short form for "extended play": a record that has more songs than a single which contains two songs; an EP usually has four to six songs

**fluent** Able to talk or communicate clearly

**international** Locations in different countries or nations

**mistrustful** Not able to trust in someone or something

**remixes** Songs that are recorded in different ways other than the original release

**spiritual** Believing in the spirit of God

**typical** Having the same qualities or characteristics of a group or type

**tween** A person younger than a teenager, usually between the ages of eight and 12

# Find Out More

## Books

*Next Step 2 Forever: My Story* by Justin Bieber, HarperCollins, 2010.

*Justin Bieber* by Sarah E. Parvis, Andrews McMeel Publishing, 2010.

*Justin Bieber: Our World* by Millie Rowlands, Orion 2010.

## Websites

Justin Bieber on Twitter
**http://twitter.com/#!/JUSTINBIEBER**

Justin Bieber on Facebook
**http://www.facebook.com/JustinBieber**

Justin Bieber: Island Def Jam Music Group
**www.justinbiebermusic.com**

Justin Bieber fansite
**http://j-bieber.org/**

# Index

## About the Author

Lynn Peppas is a writer of children's nonfiction books. She has always been a bookworm and grew up reading all the books she could. She feels fortunate to have been able to combine her love of reading and her love of kids into a career. Her work in children's publishing is a dream-job come true.